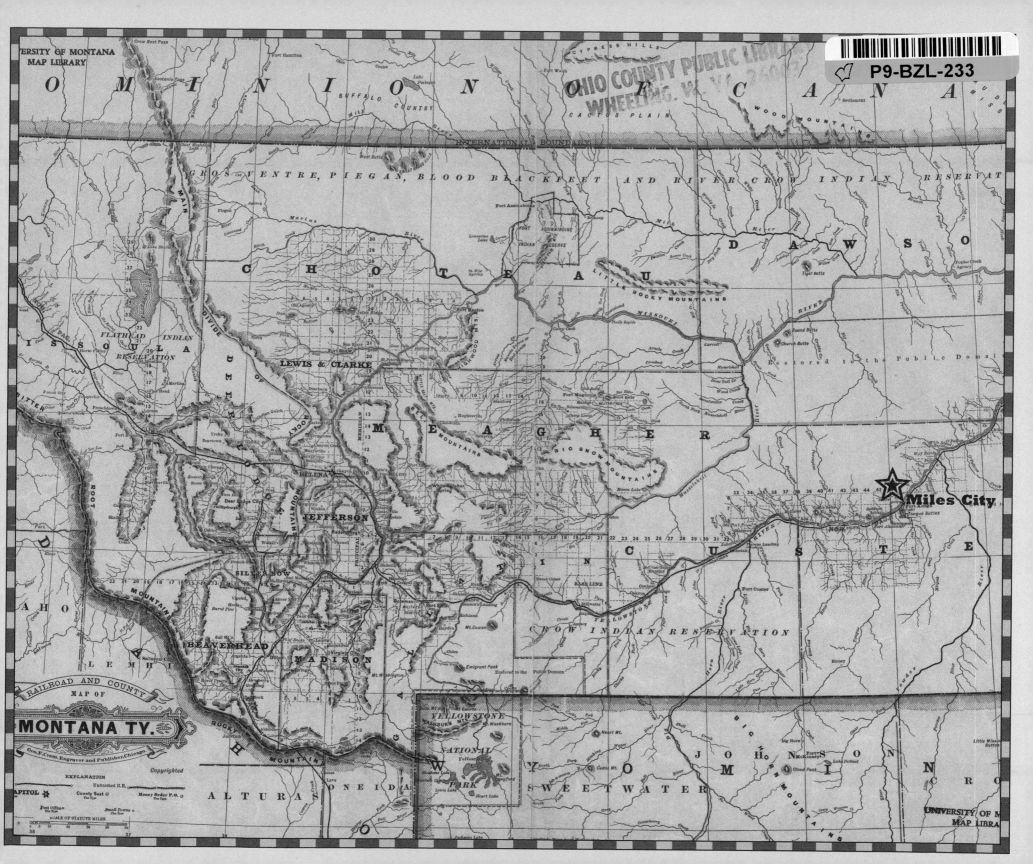

D O M I N I O N   O F   C A N A D A

CYPRESS HILLS
CACTUS PLAIN
WOOD MOUNTAIN

Crow Nest Pass
Kootanie Pass
Fort Kipp
Fort Hamilton
Fort Walsh
Settlement

INTERNATIONAL BOUNDARY

BUFFALO COUNTRY

GROS VENTRE, PIEGAN, BLOOD BLACKFEET AND RIVER CROW INDIAN RESERVAT

West Butte
SWEET GRASS HILLS

Chief Mountain Lake

Agency
Piegan
Marias River

Fort Assinaboine
FORT ASSINNIBOINE INDIAN RESERVE
Belknap
Lonesome Lake

D A W S O

LITTLE ROCKY MOUNTAINS

Tiger Butte

C H O T E A U

Fort Benton

MISSOURI   RIVER

Round Butte
Church Butte

Restored to the Public Domain

M I S S O U L A

FLATHEAD INDIAN RESERVATION

D I V I D E   O F   R O C K Y

L E W I S   &   C L A R K E

Fort Maginnis

BITTER ROOT

MONTANA

D E E R   L O D G E

HELENA

M E A G H E R

BELT MOUNTAINS

BIG SNOW MOUNTAINS

Mason Lake

JEFFERSON

MERIDIAN

C U S T E R

★ Miles City

33 34 35 36 37 38 39 40 41 42 43 44 45

SILVER BOW

GALLATIN

Bozeman
MILITARY RESERVE

BASE LINE

YELLOWSTONE

Fort Custer

D E   L E M H I

BEAVERHEAD

MADISON

Virginia City

CROW INDIAN RESERVATION

Emigrant Peak
Restored to the Public Domain

Fort McKinney

J O H N S O N

RAILROAD AND COUNTY
MAP OF

MONTANA TY.

Geo. F. Cram, Engraver and Publisher, Chicago.

Copyrighted

ROCKY MOUNTAIN

YELLOWSTONE
WASHBURN MTS
Mt. Washburn

NATIONAL
PARK
Yellowstone
Lake
Lewis Lake
Heart Lake

BIG HORN MOUNTAINS

EXPLANATION

CAPITOL
County Seat
Money Order P.O.
Post Office
Small Towns
Unfinished R.R.

SCALE OF STATUTE MILES

A L T U R A S   O N E I D A   W Y O M I N G   S W E E T W A T E R

THE WORLD FAMOUS
MILES CITY

BUCKING HORSE
S ★ A ★ L ★ E

Written and Photographed by
Sneed B. Collard III

Bucking Horse Books
MISSOULA, MONTANA

www.buckinghorsebooks.com

Distributed by Mountain Press
Mountain Press Publishing Co. • Missoula, Montana
1-800-234-5308
www.mountain-press.com

Collard, Sneed B.
The World Famous Miles City Bucking Horse Sale / by Sneed B. Collard III. — 1st ed.
        p. cm.
        Includes bibliographical references and index.
SUMMARY: Explores the drama and history of one of the West's premier rodeo and cultural events, the Miles City Bucking Horse Sale. Begun in 1951 as a way to sell "spoiled" and unruly ranch horses for use in rodeos, the sale has evolved into a four-day celebration that features horse racing, country music, a parade, and rodeo riding. Includes more than 60 photographs.
        Audience: Ages 8-14.
        LCCN 2010902149
        ISBN-13: 978-0-9844460-0-1

1. Rodeos—Montana—Miles City—History—Juvenile literature. 2. Horses—Juvenile literature. 3. Country life—Montana—Juvenile literature. 4. Miles City (Mont.)—History—Juvenile literature. [1. Rodeos. 2. Horses. 3. Country life—Montana. 4. Miles City (Mont.)—History.]   I. Title.

        GV1834.55.M92M55 2010   791.8'4'0978633
        QBI10-600037

Book design by Kathleen Herlihy-Paoli, Inkstone.
The text of this book is set in Rockwell Light.

Printed in Hong Kong

10 9 8 7 6 5 4 3 2 1

Front Cover Photos (clockwise from upper left)
1. Alice and Margie Greenough (Courtesy National Cowgirl Museum and Hall of Fame).
2. Pickup men escort "bucked out" horse from the ring.
3. Contemplating the ride.
4. Nathan Hofer covers a good bull.
5. (center panel) Yellowstone River country, eastern Montana.

Back Cover Photo: Gettin' some air.
Front Flap: The Grand Marshall and his entourage lead off the Bucking Horse Sale Parade.

All photographs by Sneed B. Collard III, except where noted.

For Amy,
Who makes everything possible.
Love, Sneed

Table of Contents

Introduction

Bustin' Out

The bareback rider adjusts his grip on the rigging one last time, then gives a nod to the men handling the gate. They yank it open and all hell breaks loose. The bucking horse bursts out of its holding pen, hooves flying, and catapults into the air. The rider's boots fling skyward while his torso slams back like a feed sack onto the horse's rump. Remarkably, the young rider hangs on, grunting with determination—or desperation—as the horse lands with a stiff-legged jolt.

But the horse is just getting started. Having failed to dislodge the annoying pest on its back, the bronc twists to the left and kicks its back legs almost vertically. Then, without pause, it launches like a NASA booster rocket, arching gracefully into the air before its front legs stab back into the earth. Still, the rider sticks with the explosive twelve hundred-pound beast beneath him. Even better, the cowboy thinks, the buzzer will sound at any moment, giving him a good riding score.

Alas, the cowboy's confidence comes too soon. In a flash of equine brilliance, the horse launches again, carrying the rider forward. Only this time, the animal doesn't continue into the air. It stops abruptly, throwing its head down.

The cowboy doesn't have a chance. His spurs fly back over his head and he somersaults with a thud into the dirt of the arena. And if this were a normal rodeo, that would be it.

★ Right and facing page: *Bucking horses have a saddle-bag full of tricks to dislodge un-wanted cowboys.*

★ Left: *The crow's nest serves as Command Central for BHS events, and is also where the auctioneer calls the sale of broncs and bulls.*

★ Facing page: *While buyers bid on it, a bucking horse runs a "victory lap" before being escorted from the ring by BHS pick-up men.*

Mounted pick up men would escort the wild buckin' bronc safely away. The cowboy would stagger to his feet and stumble, dusty and disappointed, back toward his fellow riders.

But this isn't an ordinary rodeo. Today, while the bronc takes a victory lap, an auctioneer from the crow's nest above suddenly begins firing off a blaze of machine-gun chatter over the loudspeakers.

"Sowhaddowehearforthisfierymaretodayfolksletsstartthebiddingatthree hundreddowehavethreehundredthreehundredTHREEHUNDREDdowehave fourhundredfourhundredfourhundredFOURovertotheleftletsgotofivehundred fivehundreddowehavefivehundredfivehundredfivehundred(breath) notakersatfivehundredokayhowaboutfourfiftyfourfiftyfourfifwehaveFOUR FIFTYhowaboutfourseventyfivefourseventyfivefourseventyfive…goingonceat-fourfiftygoingtwice…(breath)SOLD for four hundred and fifty dollars!"

And with that, the next rider and horse take deep breaths and prepare to burst out into the arena.

Welcome to the Bucking Horse Sale...

O r, more precisely, welcome to *The World Famous Miles City Bucking Horse Sale*. The event's grandiose name is not an idle boast. While other auctions and rodeos have come and gone, the Bucking Horse Sale has helped keep Western tradition and culture alive for more than sixty years. During that time, the sale has evolved from a simple way to sell unruly mares and geldings to a celebration of frontier and small-town life.

"It's the Mardi Gras," explains Rob Fraser, co-owner of the Miles City Livestock Commission, which runs the actual bucking horse auction.

Here, cowboy hats and boots replace the colorful masks and costumes of the New Orleans Mardi Gras, but visitors and locals look forward to the Sale with the same gusto and enthusiasm. Every third weekend in May, thousands of visitors converge on Miles City in eastern Montana. The crowd is greeted by high-energy horse racing, country music, a parade, a quick draw art competition, mutton bustin'—and some of the most exciting rodeo riding to be seen this side of, well, anywhere.

Chapter One

Concerts, Cowboys, & Cowgirls

★

It's the Wednesday before the Bucking Horse Sale and a genuine blizzard has engulfed Main Street—in May, believe it or not. Snow falls so thickly that it obscures storefronts only a block or two away. Not for the first time, Miles City residents and business owners fret that the bad weather will keep crowds at home.

They needn't worry.

By the next evening, when BHS events officially begin, the snow has moseyed on over the horizon, and forecasts call for a warm, sunny weekend.

Of course that doesn't mean that everything goes smoothly.

Concert Calamity

L ike many fairs and rodeos, the Bucking Horse Sale kicks off with a concert, this one on Thursday night. This year's event features country western star Darryl Worley, and for Worley, it's a rough ride. His plane to Billings—the nearest large airport to Miles City—is struck by lightning early in the day, and Worley is forced to hire a charter jet to get to the concert on time.

Then, halfway through his music set, a gust of wind picks up the heavy lid of an equipment case and slams it into Worley's head. Blood streams down the singer's face and medical crews rush him to the local emergency room. Remarkably, Worley returns to the fairgrounds an hour later to finish the concert—with seven stitches in his head. The singer's dedication earns him big points with his fans, but it also represents a spirit and determination typical to this part of the country— an ability to roll with the punches, and when necessary, to experiment and improvise. It's a theme reflected by the Bucking Horse Sale itself.

★ Previous page: *Even in Montana, a May blizzard creases foreheads.*

 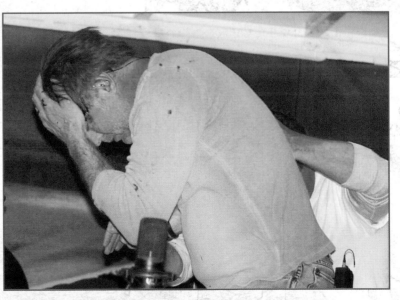

★ Above: *Before and after, a gust of wind and an equipment case lid temporarily interrupt Darryl Worley's Thursday night concert.*

Let's Have a Sale!

★ Above: *Rodeo grew out of the real skills cowboys needed to tame and manage ranch livestock.*

Two men, Les Boe and his son-in-law Bob Pauley, are credited with starting the Miles City Bucking Horse Sale back in 1951. It began as just a way to get rid of wild or "spoiled" horses that ranchers couldn't use. But the sale never would have been possible without the emergence of one of America's most popular sports: rodeo.

Rodeo didn't begin as a spectator sport, but as a way for Mexican *vaqueros* and American cowboys to perfect and show off their skills. In 1883, however, "Buffalo Bill" Cody created a Wild West show. This extravaganza, which soon began traveling across America and Europe, offered spectators a chance to experience the romance of the frontier. Cody incorporated many aspects

of rodeo into his show, and it wasn't long before similar spectacles sprang up all across the country.

As they evolved, these shows increasingly emphasized different sporting events such as bronc riding and steer roping. By the mid-1940s, hundreds of rodeos had popped up all around the U.S., and the sport's popularity rivaled that other great American pastime, baseball.

Many rodeos were large productions. They attracted the nation's top cowboys and cowgirls, who competed for cash prizes. However, the majority of rodeos were smaller community events. One thing both big and small rodeos needed was spirited bucking horses that could give cowboys and cowgirls a ride for their money. Miles City, Montana just happened to be in a perfect location to supply some of these horses.

★ Left: *"Buffalo Bill" Cody's Wild West shows gave city-bound audiences a taste of the Western frontier—and helped lay the foundations for modern rodeo.*

Wide-Open Country

The great grasslands that dominate the center of our continent have always provided ideal forage and habitat for grazing animals, including horses. "This is big wide-open dry country," explains Rob Fraser. "It has lots of good horses and always has."

10,000 years ago, in fact, horses thrived here. For reasons that are still hotly debated, those earlier horses went extinct. But when the Spanish reintroduced horses in the sixteenth

★ Facing page: *Eastern Montana's "big, wide-open dry country" still provides a perfect environment for raising and breeding horses.*

★ Left: *Fort Keogh was established to subdue the region's Indian nations. It was later converted to a remount station to supply horses for the U.S. Army and our allies during wartime.*

century, native peoples quickly recognized the animals' potential. It's no surprise that the region gave rise to powerful horse-based nations such as the Sioux, Cheyenne, Crow, and Blackfoot.

When white European Americans settled the area, horses also played a key role in their success. Army cavalry units used horses to defeat native tribes and steal their lands. Cattlemen relied on horses to manage the huge cattle herds that fueled the region's growth. Horses were also essential for farming and transportation.

Montana became so well known for horses that the U.S. Army converted Fort Keogh—outside of Miles City—into the nation's largest remount station in 1909. During World War I, more horses were acquired and trained at Miles City than at any other place in the United States. Tens of thousands of the animals were shipped to battlefronts across Europe.

In the decades after the war, the region continued to produce an abundance of top-quality horses—so many that ranchers needed a way to sell some of them.

Remount Station

A facility designed to acquire and train fresh riding horses for some purpose such as warfare, the Pony Express or, more recently, duty with the U.S. Forest Service.

The First Sale

For the 1951 Bucking Horse Sale, Bob Pauley and Les Boe collected more than a thousand horses from local ranchers. The two men held the sale in May and during a three-day period "bucked out" 350 horses per day. Bob and Les did not yet think to run the sale as a rodeo contest, but instead paid cowboys "mount money" to ride the horses for prospective buyers. A cowboy received $5 for each bareback animal he rode, and $10 for each saddle bronc ride. As soon as each horse was ridden, it was auctioned off. Even though the sale wasn't advertised as a public event, it drew a big crowd eager to watch horses get bucked out—and cowboys get bucked off.

That gave Les Boe bigger ideas.

★ Below: *As this 1971 photo shows, the Sale has never run short on action and excitement.*

"Bucking Horse Extra": A Short History of Miles City

Miles City's roots date back to the final days of the Indian Wars. After Colonel Custer's defeat at the Battle of the Little Bighorn in 1876, the U.S. military decided it had to crush the northern Plains Indian tribes once and for all. To help it gain complete control of the region, the U.S. Army built Fort Keogh, a cavalry post where the Tongue and Yellowstone rivers meet in southeastern Montana. The fort was commanded by General Nelson A. Miles, also known as the "Brave Peacock" for his courage and flamboyant good looks.

A hero of the Civil War and a veteran of the Indian Wars, General Miles used Fort Keogh as a base to harass and subdue the last of the free northern Plains Indians. Once these holdouts had been forced onto reservations, it cleared the way for vigorous Western settlement.

Originally known as "Milestown", Miles City started as a small settlement to provide services to the soldiers of Fort Keogh. Even before the Indian Wars ended, however, cattlemen began driving herds from Texas up to Montana, where an abundant supply of free grass fattened up their stock. The presence of so many soldiers and cowboys transformed Miles City into a classic Wild West town. Daily life focused on drinking, gambling, and other spirited activities. The local paper, *The Yellowstone Journal*, noted in 1880, "we have twenty-three saloons in our town and they all do a good business; we are going to have one church soon..."

Railroads gave Miles City an even bigger boost. The arrival of the Northern Pacific Railroad in 1881 and the famed "Milwaukee Road" in 1908 provided Montana ranchers with an easy way to get their livestock to eastern markets. This created an explosion of wealth in the region, and it wasn't long before Miles City became a respectable community. Electricity arrived. Fixed ranches and farms with fencing replaced the open range. The automobile began to displace the horse as a common means of transport. Today, Miles City offers eastern

Montanans every modern convenience. Like many Western towns, though, its roots still lie right beneath the surface. To discover them, all you have to do is grab a shovel and dig.

★ Below: *Miles City began as a wild frontier town, but railroads helped bring prosperity and respectability.*

The following year, 1952, Les charged $1.00 a person for admission to watch the Sale. Those who went got a special treat—a glimpse at "The Singing Cowboy", Gene Autry. In the 1940s and 50s, Autry was one of America's most famous TV and radio personalities, and also starred in more than forty "B" Western movies. Autry also ran his own rodeos and bought several bucking horses at the 1952 sale.

From then on, the popularity of the Sale grew, and organizers added additional events and features. By 1975, the three-day festivities drew 13,000 people from all around the country and even from overseas. After each day's fairground events, visitors swarmed Main Street to join in a street dance and try to capture eastern Montana's frontier spirit. Local bars served hundreds of gallons of beer in troughs and the Miles City jail filled to capacity. Extra police were brought in to keep the crowds manageable.

Since that time, the drinking has been tamed down a bit, but new activities and events have attracted a bigger variety of visitors. Today, that ability to grow and change has made the Miles City Bucking Horse Sale one of the West's must-see celebrations.

Chapter Two

If It's Bull Bustin', It Must Be Friday

⭐

Friday is when the Bucking Horse Sale kicks into high gear. The day begins mildly enough, with a pie baking—and *eating*—contest at Riverside Park. This is followed by a beer brat barbeque over at the Elks Lodge. By five o'clock, though, most serious rodeo fans are heading to the Eastern Montana Fairgrounds for the first big BHS event: bull riding.

As the clock ticks down to starting time, a sense of excitement builds in the stands. The first bull does not disappoint. Barging out of its chute, the fifteen-hundred-pound animal immediately spins, or "turns back", flinging its rider to the ground. As a horrified cry goes up from the crowd, the bull tramples the rider and then, adding insult to injury, swipes horns at the unfortunate cowboy's backside before the bullfighters rush in to the rescue. The next thirty-six bulls do not have quite the success in humiliating their riders, but do serve up tons of excitement.

No matter how well each cowboy does riding his bull, the mere fact that he does it earns respect from the crowd. Just the thought of sitting on an animal that is eight or ten times your weight and wants to *kill you* is beyond the consideration of most sane individuals. But for bull riders, taking on one of the enormous, powerful gladiators is more than fun—it's their life's blood.

A Bull Rider's Tale

At age forty-five, Robert Mims is probably the oldest bull rider in this year's competition. In mostly-white Montana, he's also the only black bull rider in sight. Robert grew up in Bryan, Texas, but moved to Billings, Montana in 1996. He was only nine years old when he caught Bull Ridin' Fever.

"My neighbor was a bull rider," he explains, "and me and my brother used to sneak over to his place and ride his cows he had in the pen. One day, he caught us and asked us what we were doin'. And I told him 'I want to be a bull rider like you.' 'Well,' he said, 'that's going to take some trainin'. 'So I ended up working as a ranch hand for the man, fifty dollars a week, and I worked for him for five months before I even had a chance to get on anything.''

Asked how he finds the courage to climb onto an animal that could crush him with a flick of its head, Robert replies, "Well, it's like me against the beast. When you're squattin' down there over the bull, your nerves and your feet and your arms are shakin'. I don't care who you are, they're still shakin'. Your heart's beatin' really, really fast, the adrenaline running through you."

The fact is that no one would do it unless he were plain crazy or just couldn't help himself. For Robert, it's the latter. "The love I got for the sport is unreal. If I've got the choice of goin' to the rodeo or goin' to my brother's wedding, I'd go to the rodeo."

Bull Riding Nuts and Bolts

A love for bull riding, though, doesn't explain *how* someone rides a bull. To earn a score, a rider must stay on his bull for a full eight seconds. That's a lot longer than you might think.

"Eight seconds seems like an eternity sometimes," Robert Mims explains, "especially when you're on a bull that's turnin' back really fast, or you got a bull that's jumpin' up in the air. It feels like time takes forever. Me, personally, I find a spot on the back of the bull's head, and that's what I'm focusin' on, watchin' that one spot."

Even experienced riders get bucked off—a lot. At a national level, most top-ranked bulls buck off their riders seventy to one hundred percent of the time. Tonight at the Bucking Horse Sale, only nine of thirty-seven riders manage to "cover" their bulls, or last the full eight seconds for a score.

For every bull rider, the threat of injury is also never far away. In 1978, the Sportswriters of America selected bull riding as the most dangerous sport in the country. "If you're ridin' bulls,"

Robert confirms, "you're supposed to get hurt sooner or later. It's not a matter of when or how bad—it's gonna happen. This last year, I broke a cheekbone up in Hamilton. A couple weeks after that, the same bull broke my sternum. He did it with his horn, and even with my protected vest, he cracked my sternum. And this same bull—his name is Brass Knuckles—I keep drawin' this bull and he keeps beatin' me up."

Robert says this with a laugh that reveals the kind of attitude you have to have if you're going to brave the bull. "My goal is just to win. I've rode Brass Knuckles six times and he's beaten me up four times. I've covered him twice, but I've never really won on him. I got a grudge match between me and Brass Knuckles."

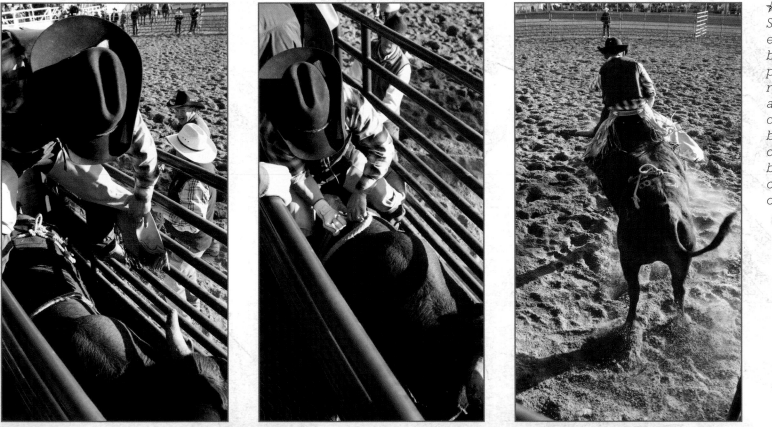

✭ Left: *Ready. Set. Go! Bull riders stay on their bulls by gripping a braided rope wrapped around the bull's chest. The cowboy's free hand cannot touch the bull at any time or the rider is disqualified.*

"Bucking Horse Extra": The Flank Strap

To encourage bulls and broncs to buck, a padded leather strap called a "flank strap" is tied around the waists of the animals. One common misconception about rodeo is that this strap is tied around the animals' genitals and that they buck because they are in pain. This isn't true. Bulls and broncs have a natural instinct to buck. The strap merely annoys or irritates the animals, encouraging their natural bucking instincts. The strap comes with a quick-release mechanism that makes it easy to undo. Cowhands release the straps on the bulls as soon as they leave the ring. For broncs, it is the mounted pick-up men (see Chapter Four) who move in and release the strap as soon as each ride is over.

★ Right: *Eleven-year-old Haven Meged stays alert to the action while collecting flank straps after each ride.*

Bull Rider 9-1-1

As Robert's experiences suggest, bull riding wouldn't be possible without people to rescue riders who have been thrown to the ground or somehow get stuck on their giant muscle-bound rides. When a rider does get in trouble, his life often depends on brave saviors who used to be called rodeo clowns. Today, they are called bullfighters.

"Once the cowboy gets off," bullfighter Shawn Penrod explains, "you gotta be there to save him. Because if he's lying there, the bull's going to come get him, throw him in the air or run over him."

Shawn used to ride bulls himself, but switched to bullfighting sixteen years ago. Since then, the Northern Rodeo Association has named him Bullfighter of the Year thirteen times. His job is to distract bulls away from riders who have gotten thrown or finished their rides.

And just how does one distract a furious, charging animal that looks like an out-of-control diesel locomotive?

"Get their attention. Either hollering at 'em or getting real close," Shawn explains. "Sometimes you slap 'em on the head or the nose, or in the ear."

Slap a bull?

"Most of the times they'll see you and they'll move away. A lot of times, they won't. They'll just run over the cowboy—run over the top—and they'll come back. You gotta be there, because they're going to throw a horn at that cowboy. What we try to do is get between the cowboy and the bull, so the bull doesn't have a choice."

Things don't always work out perfectly.

Long Go and Short Go

In rodeo, the long go, or "go round", is the preliminary round of a competition in which all entrants compete. Top riders then go on to compete in the short go, or finals.

Chute, or Rodeo Chute

A small stall or holding pen where a cowpoke outfits and mounts a bull or bucking horse before a ride.

★ Facing page: *In the battle between bull and rider, the bull usually reigns supreme.*

★ Right: *BHS chute boss Pat Linger gets young riders organized for the day's most exciting and dangerous event—mutton busting!*

"About a year and a half ago," Shawn remembers, "I had a bull slap me up against the fence and put some stitches in my forehead. A couple of weeks ago, I had to save a cowboy who got thrown here, and then the bull ran me over. I had to have sixteen staples put into the back of my head where he stepped on me."

Breaking For Mutton Bustin'

Fortunately, tonight, no bull riders or bullfighters are seriously injured—though Shawn and his fellow bullfighter, Craig Mailer, have to help more than a dozen riders to safety. Robert Mims, in fact, has a great ride, finishing third in the preliminary round, or "long go". While the top five riders gather their wits to compete in the second round, or "short go", the crowd is treated first to a sheep-shearing demonstration, and then to an event that strikes fear deep into the heart of even a brave, experienced bullfighter like Shawn Penrod—mutton bustin'!

"Ooooh," Shawn groans with a shudder. "Mutton busting is horrible!"

Mutton busting—or sheep riding—offers the littlest cowboys and cowgirls a chance to test their riding skills. Tonight, forty-three kids have signed up, but there are only enough sheep for twenty-seven to ride. Those twenty-seven give it their all. One at a time, each sheep comes stampeding out of the chute with a determined young rider clinging to its back.

The riders are treated to the same thrills and spills as the bull and bronc riders they admire. The boys and girls slide into the dirt. They are thrown to the ground. When they get in trouble, the bullfighters bravely pluck them from their

"Bucking Horse Extra": Montana's Rodeo Women

Just as Montana produces top rodeo horses and bulls, it has also produced some of the top rodeo women of all time. They include Cowgirl Hall of Famers Fannie Sperry-Steele, and Alice and Margie Greenough. Fannie, raised near Helena, was proclaimed Lady Bucking Horse Champion of the World in 1912 and 1913. The Greenough sisters of Red Lodge each won bronc riding championships in the 1930s.

All three champions grew up on Montana ranches, where they honed their skills and developed a taste for adventure. After they left home, they supported themselves by competing in rodeos, working odd jobs, and appearing in the Wild West shows that were so popular at the time. Each woman also bucked broncs in Miles City.

Long before the Miles City Bucking Horse Sale, the Miles City Roundup dominated as the town's main rodeo event. In only the second Roundup, held in 1914, Fannie Sperry-Steele won the "cowbelles" bucking horse event before a crowd that included famed Western artist Charles Russell. Years later, Alice Greenough wowed fans by riding a bronc considered by most to be unrideable.

During the time of these champions, women often competed on equal footing with men. By the 1950s, however, women had been squeezed out of mainstream rodeo competition. Hollywood celebrity Gene Autry had a lot to do with this. By the 1950s, Autry was the most important rodeo producer in the nation, and he didn't want women taking up space in his rodeos.

Women's rodeo once again flourishes today in all-girl rodeos and big-time barrel racing. As for the Bucking Horse Sale, it hasn't offered women's competition in several years, but its directors are reportedly thinking about bringing it back. When they do, it will be a welcome tribute to Montana women sporting legends.

★ Facing page: *Alice Greenough goes for a ride.*

★ Right: *Alice (left) and Margie Greenough added flair to any rodeo event.*

ferocious, grass-crazed, wool-bearin' rides. The crowd roars with admiration for every rider.

When it's all over, Gage Hart proudly raises the prize buckle for top riding honors.

But as exciting as tonight's events are, they are only a preview of the weekend to come.

★ Left to right: *Six-year-old Harley Meged describes her adrenaline-pumping ride: "Well when I first started I, um, thought he was going to rare on me and when I first got out I felt a little scared. Then I thought that when I fell off, the sheep was going to roll over on me." Fortunately, Harley survived to ride another day.*

Chapter Three
Parades and Progress

★

8:45 Saturday morning. While the previous evening's bull riders and mutton busters heal from battle, dozens, then hundreds of people begin lining Main Street, eagerly anticipating an event they've been looking forward to all spring. Finally, under the warm light of a flawless Montana sky, the air quivers with the throb of approaching drumbeats and the clip-clopping of horse hooves. Following a Miles City police car, the Parade Marshal and a dozen smartly-dressed cowboys and cowgirls ride by on groomed, gleaming horses, the riders waving to the crowd, proudly carrying American and Montana flags. The procession is greeted with a roar. The Bucking Horse Sale Parade has begun!

A Community Comes Together

Not long ago, the Bucking Horse Sale Parade featured cowboys driving the wild sale horses down Main Street. Liability issues put a stop to that, but the parade is still an event that connects Miles City residents and visitors alike. The first Bucking Horse Sale Parade was held in 1956. Since then, it has evolved into a true community celebration. Walking among the crowd, it's hard to find someone who is *not* involved in one way or another.

''My mom's a judge for the floats,'' explains third-grader Nicholas Beaner.

''I'm going to help my Momma!'' his preschool age sister Katrina joins in.

Nicholas and Katrina are students at Sacred Heart Elementary and are just two of dozens—make that hundreds—of kids participating in the event. Some hand out water to the thirsty crowd. Others roam the parade route wearing bright yellow shirts, collecting donations so that Miles City can build its first concrete swimming pool. Still others are in the parade itself, riding horses, marching and playing music, dancing Irish jigs, tossing candy from floats, and performing spine-tingling feats of balance and skill.

★ Previous page: *The bag-pipes and danc-ing of the Caledonian Society enliven an already lively parade proces-sion.*

★ Left: *Parading the Hard Way—Jamie Gierke, Madison Friend, and Toby-Jeanne Almy give it their all as part of Sacred Heart School's unicycle club.*

★ Right: *This cool quacker advertises the Rotary Club's forthcoming Rubber-Ducky Round -Up fundraiser.*

This is ten-year-old Cecelia Freese's second year riding a unicycle in the parade. She likes it, but will admit that it tests her courage. When asked if she was nervous, she exclaims, "*Really* nervous! Sometimes, when you unicycle it's really easy to fall off and hurt something. One of my friends fell off the unicycle and scraped up her knee pretty bad. So I was pretty nervous about falling."

Cecelia doesn't let that stop her from taking part. Even if she has to wobble a bit and risk kissing the pavement, she presses ahead—exactly as Miles City has done since its beginning.

Small-Town Struggles

In recent decades, Miles City has suffered through the same struggles as other rural farming and ranching communities throughout the West. As ranches and farms have grown more efficient and needed fewer hands, young people in search of education and jobs have left their communities. While other areas of the country have gained population over the past half-century, most eastern Montana towns have shrunk or disappeared altogether. Custer County's population actually peaked in the 1910 census at 14,123. By the year 2000, that figure had fallen to 11,696.

"One thing that triggered the slide back in the Sixties," explains Miles City Mayor Joe Whalen, "was the opening of the Interstate Highway. Like a lot of communities that were along what is now I-94 or I-90, as soon as the Interstate opened up, all the traffic that used to go

"Bucking Horse Extra": Rodeo Royalty

Escorting the Parade Marshal of the BHS Parade are four particularly dazzling young women—the winners of the Miss Southeastern Montana Rodeo pageant, or MSMR. They include this year's Queen Ashley Rainey, Teen Queen Bridget Gustad, Princess Kolleen Gustad, and Little Miss Katie Hoppe.

Rodeo pageants extend back as long as organized rodeo itself. One of the first was at the Pendleton, Oregon Roundup in 1910. Today, virtually all major rodeo and Western celebrations have pageants to go along with them. Unlike in the Miss America and other similar pageants, judges look at more than beauty.

"What's important," explains pageant Board member Diane Rainey, "is your basic general horsemanship knowledge and knowledge of rodeo, how well you present yourself, and your whole outlook and attitude toward keeping that Western heritage alive." For most of this year's winners, it is not prizes or tiaras that draw them to the pageant. It's a love of horses and rodeo. Queen Ashley Rainey grew up in town, but lives and breathes horses. She pursues Equine Studies

★ Left: *(left to right) MSMR winners Katie Hoppe, Ashley Rainey, and Kolleen Gustad help raise awareness of rodeo and the Bucking Horse Sale itself.*

☆ Above: *MSMR participants help lead off the BHS Parade.*

at Miles Community College. "I show a lot in the Eastern Montana Horse Show Circuit," she adds, "and then I do rodeos, just little small jackpots, and barrel racing."

Little Miss Katie Hoppe is involved in junior rodeo. "I do barrel racing, poles, goat tail tying, and dummy roping," she explains.

Goat tail tying?

"You have this little goat and you ride down on your horse as fast as you can. And you have this little ribbon and you tie it on the goat's tail," she says with a laugh.

Whatever their backgrounds, the main job of all the winners is to promote the Bucking Horse Sale and rodeo. It's a job they enjoy. When asked what her favorite part of the pageant is, Ashley Rainey answers, "Just being around little kids. Telling them all about rodeo, and getting more kids involved in it, and letting them know how fun it is."

through the Main Streets of these communities was bypassing. So we lost a lot of retail traffic through downtown."

The town reached its low point in the 1980s. In 1980, the Milwaukee Road railroad closed its operation in Miles City, laying off hundreds of workers. The region was also slammed by falling agricultural and energy prices. Even though Custer County doesn't have much gas or oil underneath it, a lot of energy services companies had set up operations in Miles City. When those companies pulled up stakes, it hit the town hard.

Miles City, though, has resources that other places don't. "We happen to be the largest population center in eastern Montana, so we're a natural retail and recreational hub for some of those other communities that are losing population," Mayor Whalen explains. In a world that seems increasingly dangerous and complex, many people are also recognizing Miles City as a great place to settle down.

"This is one of the few places in the world where you can allow your four- or five-year-old child to ride her tricycle down to the end of the block and not be overly concerned about problems. As long as that feeling is maintained, that sense of security, and as long as we've got enough of an open-space buffer between places like Gillette and Billings, we have an opportunity to really carve out a little piece of paradise here."

Those advantages have helped Miles City hold its own while surrounding communities continue to decline. Between the 1990 and 2000 census, Custer County lost exactly one person—a pretty good result for eastern Montana. That doesn't mean that Miles City citizens are sitting around waiting for good fortune to smile down on them.

Parading Out A Vision

During the past decade or two, Miles City citizens have worked hard to create a new vision for their town. They have successfully courted new businesses, beefed up Miles Community College, and grown a blossoming arts community that brings together

★ Right: *For families, smaller towns such as Miles City offer both safety and a wholesome high-quality way of life.*

musicians, artists, writers, and thespians. Most impressive, these new activities coexist with the town's traditional values and agricultural roots—all of which can be seen in the Bucking Horse Sale Parade.

"The parade, for me, is the highlight of the Bucking Horse Sale," Mayor Whalen admits. "It's a long, charismatic, community parade."

Many other Miles City residents feel the same way. Though smaller and simpler than the Macy's or Rose Bowl parades, the Miles City procession exudes a vitality, an authenticity often missing from modern life. Mixed in with horses pulling old-time wagons and the 7th Cavalry Drum and Bugle Corps blasting out a tune, people watch modern tractors and business floats, horse-riding clubs, and the soulful bagpipes and matched kilts of the Miles City Caledonian Society. Halfway through the parade, a hot rod suddenly brakes, engine screaming, to "burn rubber" in front of squealing kids.

As a cloud of vaporized rubber engulfs the street, one parent, Lori Rogers, dryly remarks, "They had to get after him for that last year."

Her remark perhaps unlocks the key to the parade: this isn't a performance to be watched. It's an expression of the entire community, reflecting not only what the region is, but what it hopes to be.

"Bucking Horse Extra": Parade Poll

While Miles City kids are almost unanimous in their excitement over the parade, this reporter wondered what the parade's best feature might be. In a highly scientific poll, he decided to ask the kids themselves:

"I'd have to say the candy and food."

—Nicholas Beaner, 3rd Grade, Sacred Heart School

"The candy."

—anonymous Kindergartner

"I don't really know."

—Quinn Rogers, 1st Grade, Garfield Elementary

"Probably when all the cars come."

—Allie Erickson, 3rd Grade, Garfield Elementary

"The fire trucks."

—Quintin Cook, 6th Grade, Garfield Elementary

"Candy. And at the Bucking Horse Sale, my favorite part is eating cotton candy."

—Brendan Cook, Kindergarten, Garfield Elementary

"I like the fire trucks. And I like handing out water."

—Matthew Donnelly, 2nd Grade, Sacred Heart School

☆ *Above: Parade candy leads to lively bartering session between Miles City resident Quinn Rogers and visitor Braden Collard.*

So there you have it. According to Miles City's next generation of voters, candy is the sweetest part of the parade, with fire trucks coming in a respectable second. The question is, will it stay that way? Will fire trucks extinguish candy? Will horses or yellow rubber ducks march into the mix? Stay tuned to Parade Polling Central to find out.

On To The Park!

★ Below: *The 7th Cavalry Drum & Bugle Corps, from Sheridan, Wyoming, has a long tradition of performing throughout the West.*

As the last of the horses, floats, bands, and tractors complete the parade route, people start streaming from Main Street over to Riverside Park. While waiting for the free barbeque thrown by the Kiwanis Club every year, kids swarm the playground and adults converge on the quick draw art competition.

At 10:30, twenty-four regional artists are given exactly thirty minutes each to complete a work of art in the medium of his or her choice. While most artists paint or draw, a couple of brave souls work in sculpture. All of the works have a Western theme, and the quality of the work is astonishing, featuring landscapes, livestock and wildlife, ranch scenes, Indian villages, and other

icons of the frontier. Even better, it's all for a good cause.

Much like the bulls and horses out at the fairgrounds, the newly-created art works are auctioned off to enthusiastic bidders. Half of the proceeds go to the artists, but the other half benefits the Custer County Art and Heritage Center. This year, the thirty-minute masterpieces bring in a good haul—$9,300, with one pastel selling for $1,000.

For many, especially families, the parade, barbeque and art auction are the highlight of the day. For others, however, the morning's events are simply a warm-up to the entire weekend's main event—the actual bucking horse sale itself.

★ Left: *Sales from the quick draw art competition benefit both the artists and the Custer County Art and Heritage Center.*

Chapter Four

Saturday Afternoon: Bucking Horse Heart and Soul

★

Saturday afternoon begins as hundreds of rodeos do all across the continent, with a Grand Entry. One by one, the MSMR winners and other dignitaries gallop out to take their places in front of the packed grandstand. As thousands of cowboy hats are removed from heads, eleven-year-old Haven Meged races around the ring carrying the American Flag and former Miss Montana, Jana LaBree Cass, belts out the National Anthem. While the last beautiful notes fade from the loudspeakers, a roar erupts from the crowd, and cowboys get ready for the bucking to begin.

Preparing For Battle

Buckin' broncs are divided into two categories, bareback and saddle broncs. "We run all the barebacks first," explains BHS secretary Lavetta Weeding. "They're just a smaller, lighter horse. That's what classifies them to be a bareback. Saddle broncs are a little bigger and a little heavier."

Watching the events from the stands is a much different experience than being down by the corrals. Spectators in the stands shift their attention from one activity to another—watching horses buck out, placing bets on horse races, guzzling ice-cold sodas or beer, then screaming as a blur of colorfully-clad jockeys and their mounts thunder toward the finish line for a race. Down by the ring, however, the cowboys are all business, their minds on the horses they will have to face. With more than a hundred horses to buck out, most of the cowboys have a long afternoon ahead of them.

"It's hurry up and wait," one cowboy remarks with a grin.

Different cowboys handle the stress of waiting differently. Some joke and laugh with each other. Others sit in small groups on their saddles or on the dusty ground, quietly talking or swapping stories and riding strategies. A few crouch by themselves, eyes hidden under the brims of hats, stoically studying the dirt beneath them.

When his name is called, a cowboy rises to his feet, picks up his saddle or rigging, and makes his way to the metal chute that holds his horse—his opponent. With the help of other cowboys or assistants, he gets his pony all geared up, then lowers himself down onto the animal. He focuses his mind on one thing and one thing only—and waits for the gate hands to open his chute.

★ Right: *For both bareback and saddle bronc riders, things can go bad in a hurry.*

Bareback Brawl

This year, bareback rider Richard Wilson has driven up to Miles City from his home in Idaho Falls. He began riding bulls after high school, but switched to bareback broncs six years ago. He comes to the Bucking Horse Sale because it's a chance to ride a lot of horses. A few years ago, he won the Iron Man award for riding the most horses—a total of eight. He explains the equipment he needs to ride:

"It's called a bareback riggin'. Basically it's a leather strap that goes around the horse's chest and has a rawhide handle built on top of it. It's a firm handle and kind of works like a

saddle horn. And so what we do is suck the strap down to the horse's withers pretty tight so it doesn't want to slip. The glove we wear has a lot of padding so when it goes into the handle, it doesn't go in there very easy. It kind of sticks and binds. That's what we call it, the *bind*."

To increase the strength of the bind, cowboys apply sticky resin to both the glove and the handle, and it's the bind—not the strength of the cowboy's grip—that usually keeps the rider on the horse. Unfortunately, a good bind can also get a cowboy into trouble. Today, for instance, Richard breaks his hand while getting thrown from his very first ride. No problem. He just wraps more tape around his injured paw and prepares for his next ride. But on that one, too, he finds trouble. This time, it's more serious.

As his horse explodes out of the chute, Richard spurs the horse's neck and begins curling his body into a loose "C" shape, preparing for the horse to buck. As he sits up, however, his rigging begins to slip. "It was tight enough for me to make my ride on," Richard says. "But then when it came time for me to sit up, I slid a little bit, and then I start-

Withers

The ridge between the horse's shoulder blades.

ed sliding more. And that's where things went bad.''

That's an understatement. As the rigging slides to the left, Richard falls with it. Because he's sliding to the left, he can't straighten his wrist enough to pull his hand out of the bind, and the next thing he knows, he finds himself hanging underneath the bronc getting trampled by horse hooves.

''That was the first time that's ever happened to me, so I mean, it made me a little nervous,'' Richard explains. ''I'm sittin' there tryin' to figure out how to get out, and horses are runnin' everywhere around me kicking me, stepping on me.''

When he sees what's happening, Richard's traveling partner leaps into the arena to help. Fortunately, the three pickup men get the horse stopped and, together, they get Richard's hand out of the bind and pull him away from the horse.

Does that stop Richard from riding his last horse?

Not a chance. He staggers back to the chutes, preparing for his last ride, though he later admits, ''I was a little loopy from gettin' knocked around.''

★ Left to Right: *Lookin' good… lookin' good… lookin' good… lookin' good— dang! Bareback rider Richard Wilson gives it his best, but today it's not quite enough.*

"Bucking Horse Extra": Racing, Montana Style

Many Bucking Horse Sale visitors come to watch and bet on horse racing. Montana has a strong horse-racing tradition, beginning with traditional Indian horse races long before white settlers moved to the region. Later, in Miles City's early days, cowboys staged horse races right down Main Street. Today, Montana's racing tradition continues. In fact, former Montana racing star Medaglia d'Oro sired the winner of this year's Preakness Stakes—one of the most prestigious horse races on the planet.

Horse racing hasn't always been successful at the Bucking Horse Sale, but this year is a banner year. Owners bring almost 170 horses to Miles City, and ninety-five of them race. The races are divided up into many different categories, reflecting the horses' ages, quality, and breed, and also the length of the race. Betting is as fast and furious as the races themselves.

"It was the best handle we've ever had for Miles City horse racing," states Don Richard, who is on the Sale's Board of Governors. The "handle" is the amount of money gamblers bet on the races, and this year it totals $42,000 for Saturday alone. And while the Bucking Horse Sale may not be the world's top racing venue, it does offer horse owners some special opportunities.

★ Left and facing page: *Horse racing—and betting—provide the main draw for many at the Bucking Horse Sale.*

"Where Montana works for racing," says Montana horse-breeder Ray Norgaard, "is for anybody, and for the small person especially, to have a test spot to try their horses out and see what they have." Horse racing has become so expensive, Ray explains, that "Mom and Pop" operations have a difficult time transporting and racing their horses. And while Miles City does attract some strong talent, it also offers an opportunity to race without going broke—especially for breeders in eastern Montana.

If your horse is good, of course, you've also got a shot at some prize money. This year at the Sale, the Quarterhorse Futurity—a race of two-year-olds—dishes out a total purse of $21,440. Not bad for a day of fun in the sun.

DoIHearThreeHunnert?

As soon as a rider rides or gets bucked off a bronc, the auctioneer begins auctioning off that horse. Buyers, scattered all around the ring, are looking for good rodeo horses. Some horses sell for a few hundred dollars, others for a couple of thousand. Some horses don't sell at all.

"It can be very confusing to the audience," explains Rob Fraser. "Some horses go out and they hog around and they look like they're really buckin' and maybe they get a few kicks in, and people go 'Wow, that was a bucker. How come he didn't bring any money?' But if you put that horse in a pro rodeo string, and a top-notch cowboy like Jesse Bail draws him and just comes after him hard, aggressively, the horse won't fire."

The need for horses that will perform consistently has changed how many and what kinds of horses are offered at the Bucking Horse Sale. When the Sale first began, almost all of the horses were wild horses or "spoiled ranch horses" that a rancher couldn't use. Today, many more of the horses are bred

★ Facing page and above: *Not all bucking horses are created equal. Some "fire" right out of the gate. Others opt for a nap.*

specifically to perform in rodeos.

"In the nineteen years I've been here," Rob says, "it's gone from maybe five percent buckin' horse-bred to fifty percent of the horses having some breeding program behind them."

In the future, Rob would like the Sale to feature even more horses that are specifically bred to buck.

Why?

For one thing, many rodeo producers are now breeding their own bucking horse stock, creating more competition—and fewer buyers—for the Sale. Having better bucking horses, though, will also attract more top-notch riders. To get a good ride, a cowboy needs a horse that really knows how to buck. "Their hind hooves have got to be extended vertically," says Rob, "and they've got to kick 'em as high as possible. And then they've got to stay in that rhythm. If they don't, they probably won't stay buckin'."

To help attract better horses and riders, Sale organizers have been putting up prizes for both the stock and the cowboys. This year, a prize of $3,000 went to the best bucking horse at the sale. Top bull and bronc riders also shared thousands of dollars of prize money. Some of this cash came from stock and cowboy entry fees, but the rest was put up by sponsors to improve the quality of the entire event.

Saddle Broncin'

During the afternoon, the Sale action pauses every hour or so for a horse race or a riding demonstration. Then, it's back to bucking. Once the bareback broncs are all bucked out, it's time to pit riders against the saddle bronc horses.

As its name suggest, saddle bronc riders sit in a saddle for their rides. This saddle has no horn or handle to grab onto. Instead, the rider uses one hand to hang onto a rope called a "buck rein" attached to the halter, under the horse's chin. Holding onto that buck rein is often the main thing keeping a cowboy from getting flung into space—as saddle bronc rider Travis Spang knows too well.

Travis is from Lame Deer, Montana and comes from a long line of rodeo athletes. "I've been around rodeo my whole life," he explains. "My great auntie, Bobby Kramer, was a saddle bronc rider. She was in the Cowgirl Hall of Fame. My grandpa Buster, he rode saddle bronc a little bit, but he was mainly a roper.

★ Left: *Eight chutes allow cowboys to gear up their horses at the same time, and keep the sale moving at a brisk pace.*

★ Right: *Ready For Launch— Travis Spang gets a little too much air during his ride.*

"Bucking Horse Extra": Confessions of a Pickup Artist

When bareback or saddle bronc riders finish their rides or get in trouble, they count on pick-up man Kyle Shaw to get them safely off their horses. Kyle began working as a pick-up man at the Sale in 1998 or 1999. Most rodeos use only two pick-up men in the arena, but because of the unpredictable nature of the horses at the Sale, Kyle works with two others to save cowboys' backsides. Working inside the arena gives him a unique view of the events.

Question: How did you learn to be a pick-up man?

Kyle: I've ridden and ranched all my life so the horse part of it was no big deal. It was just a matter of figurin' out some of the, you know, techniques and stuff like that.

Q: How do you move in when a cowboy is finishing his ride?

K: Most every horse that I've ridden has a way that it wants to work. Some horses want to be ahead and slow down and let the bucking horse catch 'em, and some horses want to come in more from the side. You don't want to get too close to 'em from behind 'cause then you get kicked.

Q: Do you always ride the same horse?

K: I have four right now that I use. Over the years, I've had a lot of horses, but for the Bucking Horse Sale I need four or five depending on how many they've got to buck out.

Q: Are the horses you ride especially trained for the pick-up job?

K: We use 'em for all of our ranch work, too, but not every horse will do the pickin' up job. Other horses throwin' a fit scares a lot of horses.

Q: Is there a different approach with the bareback riders versus the saddle bronc riders?

K: Not necessarily. The bareback riders are more apt to get in trouble because of the way they tie themselves to the horse. Saddle bronc riders, the only thing really holding them down on the horse is the buck rein, or halter rope. If they turn loose of that, they're kind of free wheelin' and they don't last very long.

Q: Do you ever get nervous working as a pick-up man?

K: I guess I'd have to say that with the bareback ridin', which is where guys get in more trouble, sometimes I get excited beforehand. (With bareback) there's a little more demand on you and your horse to keep a guy out of serious trouble. In saddle bronc ridin', once in a while a guy hangs a foot in the stirrup, but saddle bronc riders—normally, if they've been doin' it very much—they wear boots that will come off and turn 'em loose. Bareback riders have their hand stuck in the bind. They can get tied to the horse and can't get out without help.

☆ Below: *BHS pick-up men help yet another cowboy to safety after his ride.*

When he was seventy-three years old, he won at (roping in) the Crow Fair, one of the biggest Indian rodeos in the world."

Travis has continued the family tradition. He's spent many years competing on the Indian rodeo circuit, and has come close to making the Indian National Finals Rodeo. This year, he's driven to the Bucking Horse Sale to tune up his skills for the coming rodeo season. For him, and most other bronc riders, nothing quite compares to climbing on that horse.

"I always get excited," Travis says. "The cool thing about it, though, is when I get on, everything calms down and it's the safest place in the world. No worries. Nothing. All of my worries just go away and I concentrate on what I got to do."

Staying on a bronc for a full eight seconds, however, requires a delicate balance of concentration and relaxation. Describing one ride the previous year, Travis recalls, "I did really good and right at the end of my ride, I just hit the front end and relaxed, and the horse, he just picked me up and bucked me off before the whistle blew. I was that close." Travis laughs appreciatively at the memory. "There was no reason for him to buck me off either. I just relaxed and afterward thought 'Oh, maaaaan!'"

Unfortunately, Travis doesn't fare any better today. After waiting all afternoon for his ride, Travis bursts out of the chute, a four-legged mass of muscle beneath him. Everything looks good at first. The horse bucks a couple of times and Travis stays with it. Then, suddenly, the horse sends the cowboy flying.

Chock up another one for the horse in the competition between man and beast.

Chapter Five

Ridin' Into the Sunset

✦

Even after the last horse is bucked out and sold, and the last traditional horse race has run, the day is still not over. Down next to the arena, a final group of untamed and unruly horses are loaded into the chutes. Only a few feet away, nervous, three-person teams of cowpokes assemble for the ultimate human versus horse grudge match: the wild horse race.

When everyone is ready, the gates to the chutes fling open at the same time, and the cowboys rush in to meet their matches. Each team's goal is to grab the buck rein of its horse, calm it down enough to get the saddle on it, and then ride the horse completely around

the fairgrounds track. It's even tougher and more dangerous than it sounds.

Within moments, cowboys are being kicked, dragged through the dirt, flung up against the chutes, and run over. One team seizes the rope of its horse and wrestles it to the ground. Seconds later, the horse kicks free and gallops away, the cowboys chasing madly after it. It takes five minutes of mayhem before one of the teams even gets its horse saddled. The rider leaps on and the crowd cheers, but

★ Left: *Three-person wild horse race teams tense before their horses burst out of the chutes.*

★ Below: *Game on!*

★ Previous page: *As the Bucking Horse Sale winds down, visitors take memories with them—and dream of returning next year.*

★ Right: *The Texas Club team rider manages to control his wild mount before heading around the track.*

their cheers quickly turn to a collective gasp. With a kick and a twist, the horse flings both cowboy and saddle to the ground, forcing the team to start from scratch.

A couple of minutes later, the Texas Club team gets a rider onto its horse. The pair buck and gallop wildly around the ring once, then head out onto the track—and in the right direction! Seconds later, the BGB family team rider heads out too. As he gallops around the track, the Texas Club rider doesn't think he's being followed, but halfway around he happens to glance behind him. He sees the BGB rider and puts spurs to his horse. Suddenly, it's a real horse race!

As the two teams gallop down the final stretch, a roar rolls out over the track. The BGB rider gains steadily and Texas Club looks like it might get overtaken. Coming around the final turn, fans scream and shout for their favorites. At the finish line, though, Texas manages to hang on, grinning and waving, to win by a couple of lengths.

Whoopin' It Up and Windin' Down

After the wild horse race, the grandstands empty. Most people head downtown for a street dance—and some serious socializing. They can afford to stay out late, because Sunday's horse races and matched bronc riding don't kick off until 1 p.m. For the cowboys especially, it's a perfect time to relax, visit with friends, and recount the day's victories and defeats.

Others will use the evening to get rested and pack up for the long drive home in the morning. Even though many insist that Sunday's matched bronc riding contest is not to be missed, some will have to return to the Bucking Horse Sale another time to experience it all. It's a pleasant thought.

Fortunately, this unique Western event promises to stick around for a long time. Although the actual sale of the bucking horses and bulls will certainly change as rodeo and the livestock market continue to evolve, the event has become a central feature in Miles City's year.

Community Glue

One of the strengths of the Sale is that it means many different things to different people. For business owners, it brings in a welcome infusion of cash.

"We look forward to the Bucking Horse Sale. We get lots of people in town," explains Mary Lou Deibel, who with her husband Jack, owns Miles City Saddlery—a one-stop shop for custom saddles, Western clothing, and just about anything else a cowboy or cowgirl could want. "It's a big part of our business, kind of like a Spring Christmas. Our Christmas season is probably our best season, and the Bucking Horse Sale ranks right up there."

For many others, the importance of the event is more social and personal.

"Particularly after harsh winters," explains Mayor Joe Whalen, "it traditionally is a time for friends and family to come back to Miles City. For most small rural Western communities, that

Matched Bronc Riding

A rodeo event in which top-ranked cowboys are invited to ride some of the best bucking horses available.

★ Right: *Retail sales during the BHS help Miles City Saddlery and many other businesses make it through the year.*

happens during the fair. Here it primarily happens during the Bucking Horse Sale because it is an opportunity for people to come to our community and just for four days drop all other cares in the world."

To have a large event like this is especially important in a smaller community. "There's not a lot to do around here," says parent Lori Rogers, "so this is a big event. The kids get to go out and do things and see everybody, and there's stuff to do. They'd miss it if it wasn't here."

Of course, Miles City residents aren't the only ones who'd miss the Sale. There's a reason why the event is called the *World Famous* Miles City Bucking Horse Sale. Thousands of visitors from every state and dozens of countries have visited eastern Montana to get a taste of the Old West.

"It's kind of an indication of what used to be every day in this country," explains rancher and local historian Bob Barthelmess. "A long time ago, there were rodeos at all big ranches every morning when cowboys mounted those son-of-a-guns that they were going to use in the day's work. If you can filter out the artificial things in the Bucking Horse Sale, the rest of it is kind of an

indication of how life was led in this country from, oh, 1885 on up through the early 1930s and even later than that."

Of course, for the cowboys that come to the Sale, it's not just about nostalgia. It's about their real lives now—an opportunity for them to pursue their dreams, make some money, and have fun at the same time.

"I really love going up there," Richard Wilson says, "so my traveling partners from this year went up there with me and they got on bareback as well, and we just went up and had a good time, and rode some horses. Sadly, none of us got any money out of the weekend, but we had a lot of fun."

All of these voices make it clear that there's not any one thing that makes the World Famous Miles City Bucking Horse Sale work. Its success lies in a rich blend of history, adventure, sport, agriculture, business, and more than anything, people. In a region of the country that is often overlooked and ignored, the Bucking Horse Sale remains part of a vibrant present—and a promising future. That, more than anything, will help it keep its reputation as one of the most interesting and entertaining celebrations in the West.

★ Left: *Rancher and historian Bob Barthelmess has deep roots in Miles City. His father settled in the area after serving in the army at Fort Keogh.*

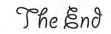

Much Obliged!

This book was made possible exclusively by the generosity of the Miles City community and the sense of welcome, enthusiasm, and cooperation extended to me and my family. It would be downright impossible to thank everyone who helped me during my visit and the writing process, but I'd like to make an effort to list the key players. First and foremost, I must thank Hannah Nash and the staff of the Miles City Public Library not only for inviting me, but for arranging my visit to coincide with the Bucking Horse Sale. Thank you! Next, I want to thank the dozens of children who shared with me their thoughts and spirit about living in one of the great towns of the West—and who put up with my many annoying questions about, well, everything!

Many people specifically made it easier to participate in the Sale and research this book. These include the Miles City Chamber of Commerce; Steve Allison, Josh Samuelson, and the staff of the *Miles City Star*; Bucking Horse Sale Secretary Lavetta Weeding; writer and artist Shelley Freese & her daughter Cecelia; the Rainey family; Rob Fraser & Bart Meged of the Miles City Livestock Commission; Mayor Joe Whalen; Bob Barthelmess of the Range Riders Museum; Amorette Allison of the Miles City Preservation Office; rodeo experts Robert Mims, Shawn Penrod, Kyle Shaw, Travis Spang, and Richard Wilson; Ray Norgaard; Mutton Bustin' coordinator Sharon Hatley; Mary & Jack Deibel of Miles City Saddlery; Misty, Haven, and Harley Meged; Nyoka Twitchell; Lory Morrow at the Montana Historical Society; Mark Fritch and Carlie Magill at the University of Montana's Mansfield Library; Tricia Dixon at the National Cowgirl Museum and Hall of Fame; photo journalists Mark Kron, George Larson Jr., John Moore, and John Riggs; Missoula librarian Karen Gonzales; and last but not least, John Scheuering, owner of Discovery Pond, the coolest kids' store in eastern Montana!

Additional thanks go out to Katrina and Nicholas Beaner, Lori and Quinn Rogers, Katie Hoppe, Ally Erickson, Quintin Cook, Brendan Cook, Matthew Donnelly, Joe Young, Amy Lancaster, Gladys and Makayla Quinlan, Larry Rothwell, Clint Griffith, and Shirley Smith.

Another special thanks to everyone at Mountain Press and Mantec for walking me through the production process.

As always, I owe a big thanks to my writer's group—Jeanette, Bruce, Dorothy, and Peggy. Special thanks to Wendy Norgaard for training her expert eye on the manuscript during final preparation—and to Kathy Herlihy-Paoli of Inkstone Design for turning this book into a work of art.

Finally, I'd like to thank my wife, son, and daughter for accompanying me on a great Montana adventure and sharing with me their ideas and enthusiasm for "Going to Miles City!"

For Further Learnin'

BOOKS

Remarkably few good books have been written about rodeo for young people. Several adult books, however, are well within the grasp of those interested in the topic. Two that I enjoyed are *American Rodeo: From Buffalo Bill to Big Business* by Kristine Fredriksson (Texas A&M University Press, 1985) and *Cowgirls of the Rodeo: Pioneer Professional Athletes* by Mary Lou LeCompte (University of Illinois Press, 1993). For personal portraits of rodeo riders, I enjoyed Margot Kahn's *Horses That Buck: The Story of Champion Bronc Rider Bill Smith* (University of Oklahoma Press, 2008). You might also try *Fried Twinkies, Buckle Bunnies, & Bull Riders: A Year Inside the Professional Bull Riders Tour* by Josh Peter (Rodale Press, 2006) or *Rodeo Legends: 20 Extraordinary Athletes of America's Sport* by Gavin Ehringer (Globe Pequot Press, 2003).

Two excellent children's books by Dorothy Hinshaw Patent explore the relationship between Native Americans, horses, and buffalo. They are *The Buffalo and the Indians—A Shared Destiny* (Clarion Books, 2006) and *The Horse and the Plains Indians : A Powerful Partnership* (Clarion Books, 2011). For a nice concise history of European invasion of Indian lands in Montana, I recommend Michael Crummett's *Tatanka-Iyotanka: A Biography of Sitting Bull* (Western National Parks Association, 2002).

VIDEOS

For the "big picture" of Western settlement, I highly recommend Ken Burns' eight-part PBS special *The West*.

A video that provides some insights into the actual Sale is *Last Stronghold: The Miles City Bucking Horse Sale*.

Two new videos by Sitting Bull's great grandson, Ernie LaPointe, give terrific new information and viewpoints on the Battle of the Little Big Horn and the theft of Indian lands. The videos are *The Authorized Biography of Sitting Bull by his Great Grandson, Parts One and Two*. These are available from the company Reel Contact.

WEBSITES

A lot of cool information about rodeo, history, and the West can be found on the web. Here are a few sites I especially enjoyed:

http://www.milescity.com/history/
Includes several wonderful histories of Miles City and surrounding areas.

http://www.prorodeo.com/
Website of the Professional Rodeo Cowboys Association, offers a wealth of information including ranks, schedules, and videos.

http://www.cowgirl.net/
This National Cowgirl Hall of Fame website is loaded with research on the best cowgirls of all time.

http://www.nationalcowboymuseum.org/ The National Cowboy and Western Heritage Museum website is a useful place to learn about many aspects of western life and events.

★ Left: *Saddle bronc rider Travis Spang jokes with an admirer before his ride.*

Western Words

Barrel Racing—a rodeo event in which a horse and rider try to complete a cloverleaf-shaped course around fixed barrels in the shortest amount of time.

Bind—the tight fit that helps keep a bareback rider's hand locked on the handle of his rigging.

Buck Out—to perform as a bucking horse, especially an untested one.

Buck Rein—a thick rope attached to an 'O' ring on the underside of a horse's halter, under the animal's chin.

Bullfighter (Bullfighting)—in rodeo, a person responsible for protecting a bull rider by distracting a bull after the rider has been thrown.

Chute—the small stall where a bucking horse or bull waits and is "geared up" before its ride.

Cover—in rodeo, to ride a full eight seconds on a bronc or bull.

Crow's Nest—a raised office or box overlooking a rodeo ring.

Dummy Roping—a rodeo event in which children test their skills roping, or throwing a lasso around, a fixed object, or dummy.

Equestrian Studies—the study of horses and horseback riding.

Flank Strap—a padded leather strap tied around a bull or bronc. The strap is designed to irritate the animal, encouraging its natural bucking instincts.

Futurity—a horse race for two year-olds, in which horses are entered before their birth.

Gelding—a castrated male horse.

Goat Tail Tying—a rodeo event in which children ride up to a tethered goat, dismount, and tie a ribbon to the goat's tail.

Grand Entry—the opening ceremonies of each day's rodeo events.

Handle—the amount of money bet on a horse race or a day of horse races.

Halter—headgear, usually made of leather or canvas straps, attached to the head of a horse or other livestock. It is most often used by a person on the ground to lead the animal by means of a rope, or buck rein, and does not involve a bit inserted into the animal's mouth.

Jackpot—a cash prize made up of the competitors' entry fees.

Long Go—the preliminary round of a rodeo event, in which all competitors compete.

Mare—an adult female horse.

Matched Bronc Riding—a rodeo event in which top-ranked cowboys are invited to ride some of the top bucking horses available.

Mount Money—a fee paid to a cowboy or cowgirl to ride a horse or bull, to show prospective buyers what that animal can do.

Pick-up Men—mounted horsemen whose job is to rescue bronc riders that are in trouble, remove them from their horses, and guide broncs out of an arena after a ride.

Poles, or Pole Bending—a timed rodeo event similar to barrel racing in which riders and horses complete a circuit around preset poles. Penalties are given for poles that are knocked over.

Remount Station—a facility designed to acquire and train fresh riding horses for some purpose such as warfare or the Pony Express.

Rigging—a strap with a handle built into it that allows a rider to hang onto a bareback bronc.

Rodeo String—a collection of stock (bulls and/or bucking horses) taken to a rodeo by a rodeo producer.

Short Go—the final round of a rodeo competition, in which top riders from the long go compete for prizes.

Stock (Livestock)—horses, cattle, sheep and other animals used and raised on a ranch or farm.

Turn Back—in rodeo, to spin, especially by a bull.

Wild Horse Race—in rodeo, a competition in which teams try to saddle and ride wild or bucking horses.

Wild West Show—a show, popular in the late 1800s and early 1900s, that sought to recreate the culture, history, and excitement of the Western frontier.

Withers—the ridge between the horse's shoulder blades.

Index

Photo Credits

Page 10: Darryl Worley photos by Steve Allison.

Page 11: "Bow Gun Series—Bucking Bronco", by L/A. Huffman. Courtesy of The Montana Historical Society Research Center, The Montana Historical Society, Helena, Montana.

Page 12: "Buffalo Bill and 101 Ranch Wild West combined Cowboys and Native Americans in formation." Courtesy Buffalo Bill Historical Center, Cody, Wyoming.

Page 14: Photo by Christian Barthelmess. Courtesy of The Montana Historical Society Research Center, The Montana Historical Society, Helena, Montana.

Page 15: Photo by Mark Kron.

Page 17: "Miles City Parade" by L.A. Huffman. Courtesy of The Montana Historical Society Research Center, The Montana Historical Society, Helena, Montana.

Page 26 & 27: Photographers unknown. Courtesy of the National Cowgirl Museum and Hall of Fame, Fort Worth, Texas.

Endpaper maps: courtesy of Archives and Special Collections, Mansfield Library, University of Montana, Missoula.